info buzz

Paramedics

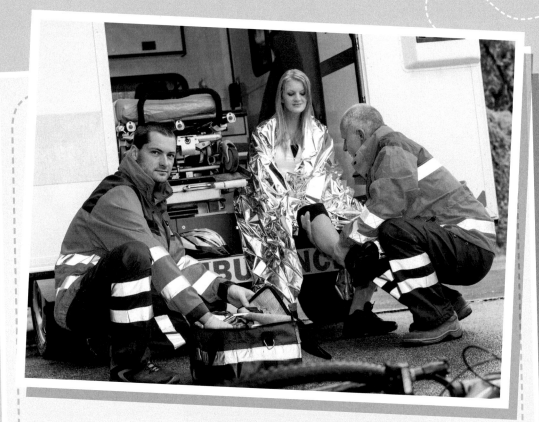

Izzi Howell

W

FRANKLIN WATTS
LONDON • SYDNEY

Franklin Watts

First published in Great Britain in 2018 by The Watts Publishing Group

Copyright © The Watts Publishing Group, 2018

Produced for Franklin Watts by
White-Thomson Publishing Ltd
www.wtpub.co.uk

ISBN: 978 1 4451 6495 3

10 9 8 7 6 5 4 3 2 1

Credits
Series Editor: Izzi Howell
Series Designer: Rocket Design (East Anglia) Ltd
Designer: Clare Nicholas
Literacy Consultant: Kate Ruttle

The publisher would like to thank the following for permission to reproduce their pictures: Getty: sturti cover and 8, FangXiaNuo 4, 13 and 14, BrianAJackson 7, kali9 9, Eureka_89 10, Zero Creatives 15, PomInOz 16t, Pengranger 16b, joegolby 17, AlexSava 18, chrispecoraro 19, Rawpixel 20, lisafx 21b; Shutterstock: CandyBox Images title page, 5 and 12, photka 6, thelefty 11, YAKOBCHUK VIACHESLAV 21t. –

Every attempt has been made to clear copyright. Should there be any inadvertent omission please apply to the publisher for rectification.

Printed in China

Franklin Watts
An imprint of
Hachette Children's Group
Part of The Watts Publishing Group
Carmelite House
50 Victoria Embankment
London EC4Y 0DZ

An Hachette UK Company
www.hachette.co.uk
www.franklinwatts.co.uk

All words in **bold** appear in the glossary on page 23.

Contents

Who are paramedics?

Paramedics look after people who are very ill or badly hurt. They help them until they can see a doctor.

◀ **Paramedics work in pairs or in groups.**

4

Paramedics drive some **patients** to **hospital** in an ambulance.

Paramedics look after the patient in the ambulance.
▼

Have you ever been inside an ambulance? What was it like?

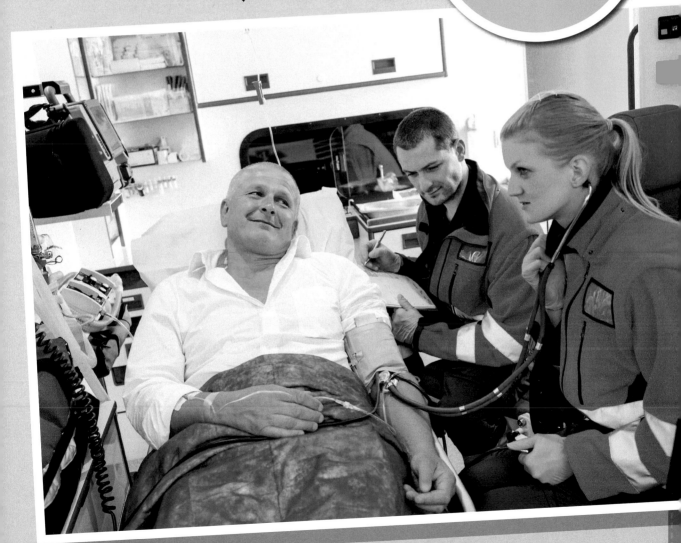

Emergency!

Calling...

999

People call for an ambulance if someone is very ill or badly hurt. In Australia, the phone number for the ambulance is 000.

◀ **In the UK, people ring 999 in an emergency.**

Paramedics drive quickly to an emergency in the ambulance. The ambulance has flashing lights and a **siren**.

The ambulance's flashing lights and siren tell other drivers to let the ambulance go in front of them.

▼

What noise does an ambulance's siren make?

On the scene

Paramedics check the patient when they arrive. They might give them **medicine** to stop them hurting.

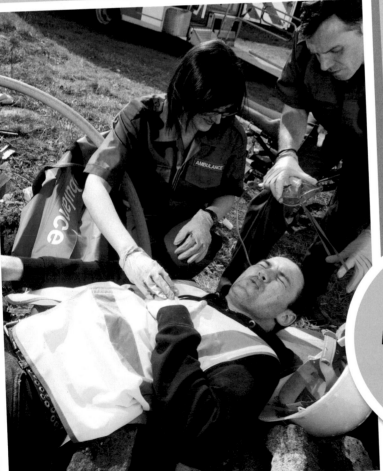

◀ These paramedics are checking on a man who has fallen.

What do you think the paramedics are saying to the man?

Some patients
are too hurt or
too ill to walk.
Paramedics
move them on
a **stretcher**.

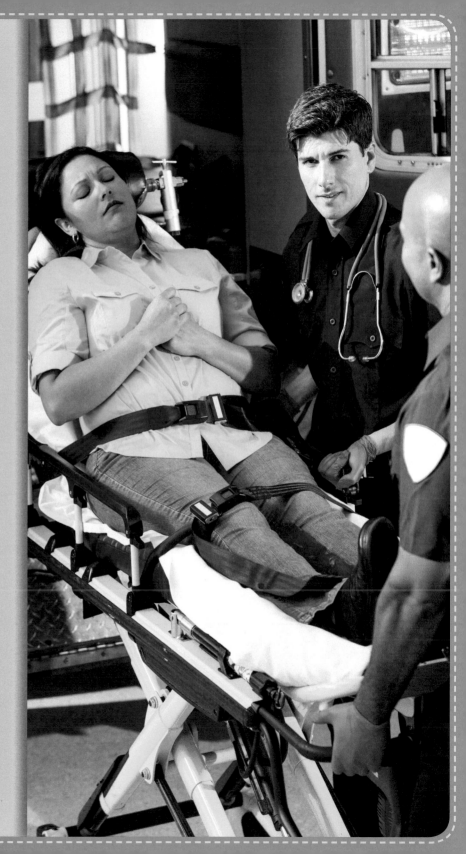

**Paramedics move
the patient into
the ambulance
on a stretcher.** ▶

The ambulance

There are machines inside the ambulance. The paramedics use the machines to **treat** patients.

▲
Medicines and **equipment** are kept on the walls of the ambulance.

Patients sit or lie on a bed in the ambulance.
A paramedic can sit next to them.

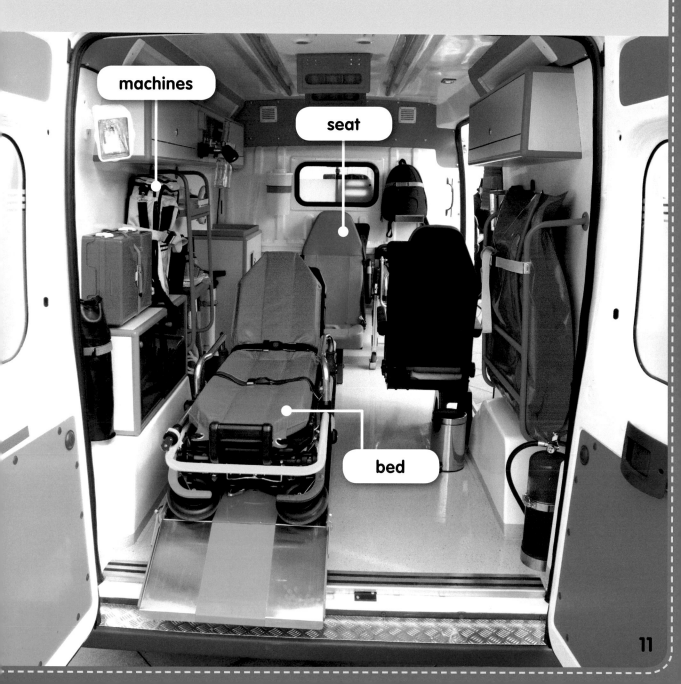

machines

seat

bed

Treating patients

Paramedics decide if a patient needs to go to hospital. Some patients can go home after being treated in the ambulance.

This woman fell off her bike. She can go home because she isn't badly hurt.

▼

Have you ever fallen off a bike? What happened?

Some patients need to go to hospital.
One paramedic treats the patient
in the back of the ambulance. The other
paramedic drives them to the hospital.

This patient is taking medicine
through a tube in the ambulance. ▼

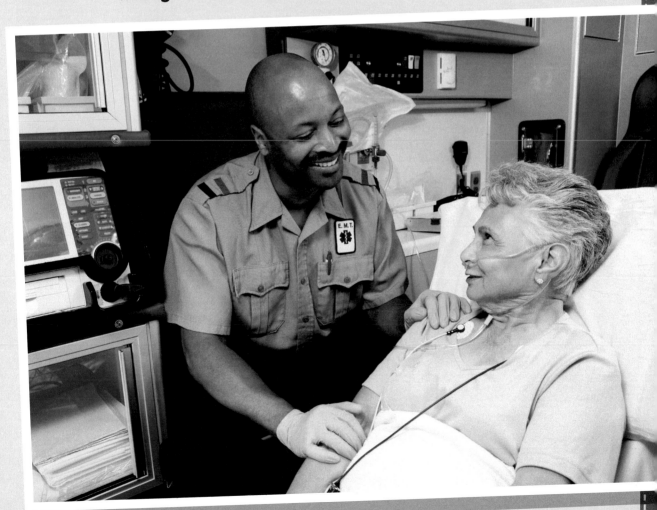

At hospital

Paramedics take the patient into the hospital. Doctors and nurses will look after the patient in hospital.

The paramedics take the patient into the hospital on a stretcher.

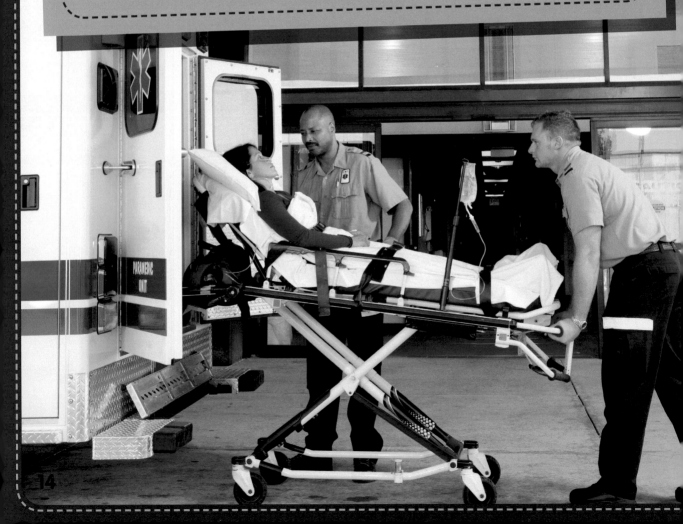

The paramedics clean the ambulance so that it is ready for the next patient. Then, they wait for another emergency call.

Every part of the ambulance needs to be clean.
▼

Why do you think the ambulance needs to be clean?

First responders

First responders are paramedics
who try to get to an emergency first.
They drive motorbikes or cars.

◀ **A paramedic can drive through traffic quickly on a motorbike.**

These paramedics on bikes are helping during a race. ▶

Sometimes, first responders treat patients by themselves. Other times, they need the help of paramedics in an ambulance as well.

▲
First responders carry some medicines and equipment.

Air ambulances

Sometimes, there are emergencies in places that are hard to reach by road. Special paramedics fly to these people in helicopters or aeroplanes called **air ambulances**.

This air ambulance is flying to help someone high in the mountains. ▶

Which other places would be hard to reach by road?

Air ambulances can travel much faster than a normal ambulance. They take very sick people to hospital quickly.

◀ Paramedics help the patient on the ground. Then, they fly them to hospital in the air ambulance.

First aid

First aid is how to help someone who is sick or hurt. We can do first aid to help in an emergency before the paramedics arrive.

This man has hurt his knee. The woman is making sure he keeps his leg still.

▼

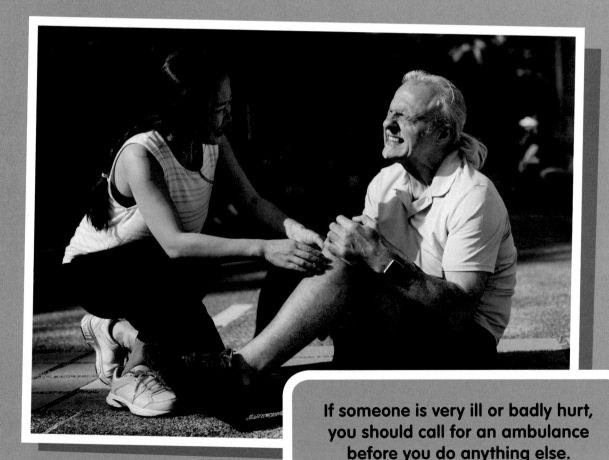

If someone is very ill or badly hurt, you should call for an ambulance before you do anything else.

We can learn some easy first aid on our own. We need special **training** to do difficult first aid.

Easy first aid – if you cut yourself, you should wash the cut and put a plaster on it. ▶

▲ These children are learning how to help someone who has stopped breathing. They are practising on a plastic model.

Quiz

Test how much you remember.

Check your answers on page 24.

1 What is the phone number for the ambulance?

2 Why do ambulances have a siren?

3 What is inside an ambulance?

4 What do paramedics do after leaving a patient in hospital?

5 What is a first responder?

6 What vehicles are used as air ambulances?

Glossary

air ambulance – a helicopter or plane that carries paramedics and is used as an ambulance

emergency – an important or dangerous situation that people need to sort out quickly

equipment – things that are used for an activity or job

first aid – the first things to do to help someone who is hurt or ill

hospital – a place where hurt or ill people are treated by doctors and nurses

medicine – something that a hurt or ill person takes or uses to make themselves feel better

patient – someone who is being cared for by a doctor

siren – something that makes a loud sound

stretcher – a flat surface used to carry someone ill or hurt

training – being taught how to do a job or activity

treat – to try and make better someone who is hurt or ill

Index

Answers:

1: 999/000; 2: To let other drivers know that the ambulance needs to go in front of them; 3: A bed, machines, medicine and equipment;4: Clean the ambulance and wait for the next call; 5: A paramedic who tries to get to an emergency first; 6: Helicopters and aeroplanes

Teaching notes:

Children who are reading Book band Gold or above should be able to enjoy this book with some independence. Other children will need more support.

Before you share the book:

- Talk about children's prior knowledge and experience of paramedics, emphasising their role in helping doctors to keep people healthy.
- Check that children have a good understanding of the idea of 'emergency'.
- If any children have ever been in an ambulance, or know someone who has, invite them to share their experiences if appropriate.

While you share the book:

- Help children to read some of the more unfamiliar words.

- Talk about the questions. Encourage children to make links between their own experiences and the information in the book.
- Discuss the pictures, talking about what the paramedics are doing and why. Talk about the equipment they are using.
- Talk about how paramedics would take people to hospital near where you live.

After you have shared the book:

- Talk about when you might call an ambulance.
- If possible invite a paramedic to come and talk to the class and show the children what the inside of an ambulance looks like.
- Work through the free activity sheets at www.hachetteschools.co.uk

People who help us

Doctors

978 1 4451 6493 9

Who are doctors?
Making an
appointment
The appointment
Instruments
Getting better
Good health
Accident and
emergency
Staying in hospital
Specialists

Firefighters

978 1 4451 6489 2

Who are firefighters?
Emergency!
Fire engines
Uniform
Rescuing people
Equipment
Trapped people
The fire station
Fire safety

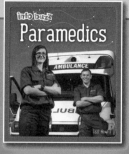

Paramedics

978 1 4451 6495 3

Who are paramedics?
Emergency!
On the scene
The ambulance
Treating patients
At hospital
First responders
Air ambulances
First aid

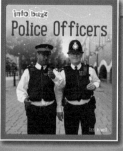

Police Officers

978 1 4451 6491 5

Who are police
officers?
Uniform
On patrol
999
The crime scene
Evidence
The police station
Vehicles
Animals

Islam

Religion

Christianity
978 1 4451 5962 1
Hinduism
978 1 4451 5964 5
Islam
978 1 4451 5968 3
Judaism
978 1 4451 5966 9

Queen Elizabeth II

History

Neil Armstrong
978 1 4451 5948 5
Queen Elizabeth II
978 1 4451 5886 0
Queen Victoria
978 1 4451 5950 8
Tim Berners-Lee
978 1 4451 5952 2

Japan

Countries

Argentina
978 1 4451 5958 4
India
978 1 4451 5960 7
Japan
978 1 4451 5956 0
The United Kingdom
978 1 4451 5954 6

FRANKLIN WATTS